The New York City Book of Cartoons

Featuring Cartoons From
Barron's
Air Mail
The New Yorker
and more!

Front Cover illustration: Charlie Hankin
Back Cover illustration: Mick Stevens
Introduction: Bob Mankoff
Design: Darren Kornblut

Cartoon Collections, LLC
10 Grand Central, 29th Floor
New York, NY 10017

For cartoon licensing information visit www.cartoonstock.com

First edition published 2024

Item # 48036
ISBN: 978-1-963079-12-8

Introduction

Greetings fellow aficionados of wit and urban charm! Welcome to the vibrant metropolis of illustrated humor with a touch of New York flair. As your humble guide, I present to you a delightful compendium of cartoons capturing the essence, eccentricities, and endless allure of the Big Apple.

If there's one thing New York City isn't short on, it's character. From the bustling streets of Manhattan to the charming corners of Brooklyn, the city is a living, breathing cartoon in its own right. And who better to capture its quirks, its idiosyncrasies, and its ever-moving pulse than cartoonists Roz Chast, Leo Cullum, Joe Dator, Emily Flake, Ellias Rosen and their fellow colleagues!

Prepare to embark on a journey through the heart of New York—a journey filled with laughter, insight, and a healthy dose of urban absurdity. Whether you're a lifelong resident, a wide-eyed newcomer, or simply an admirer from afar, this collection promises to entertain, enlighten, and perhaps even inspire.

After all, if you can make it here, you can make it into a cartoon here, too. Welcome to the ultimate cartoon tour of the greatest city on Earth!

"It's not high-definition anything. It's a window."

1

"Today is the first day of the rest of our lives in garbage."

CHATFIELD

"Max! Oh, my God! There's like a billion movie ideas in there!"

"So, who won today—you or New York City?"

"Sorry, y'all—no locals. This is a tourists-only bar."

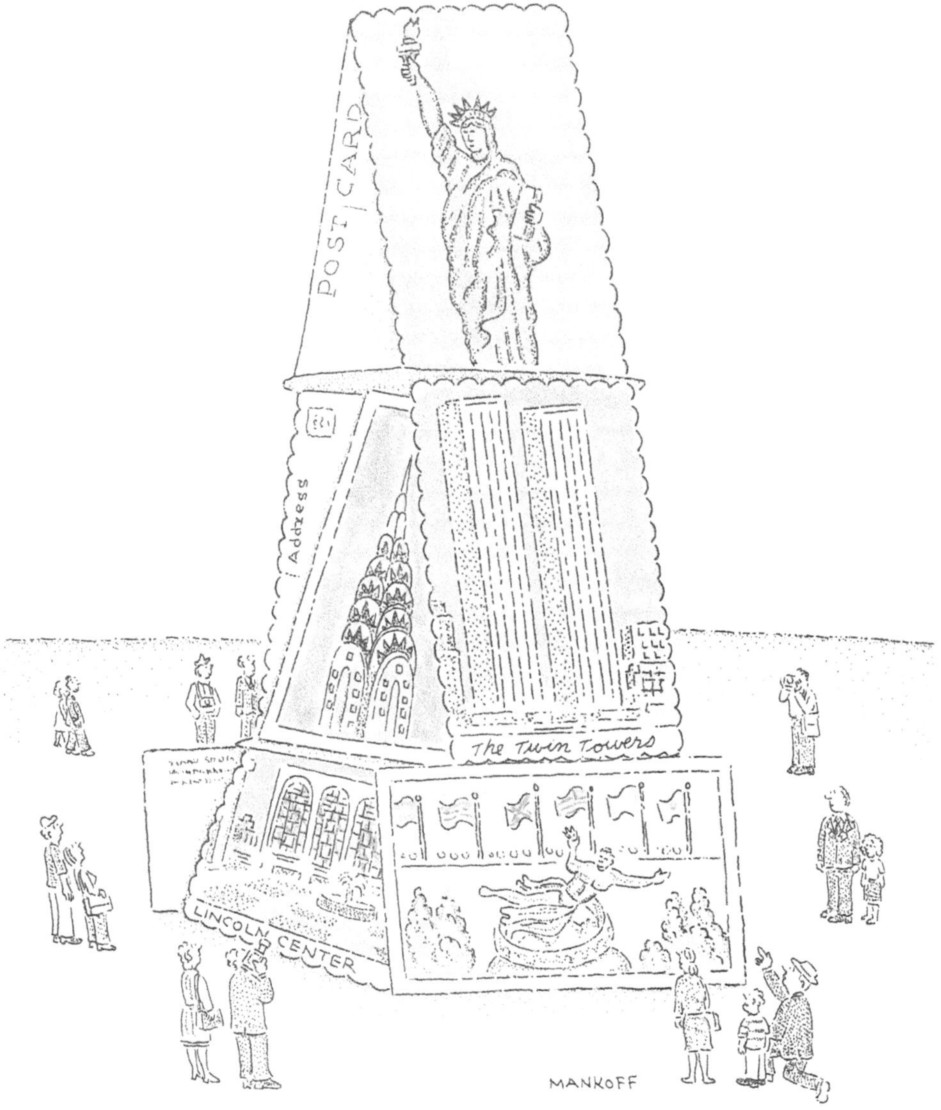
POST CARD
Address
The Twin Towers
LINCOLN CENTER
MANKOFF

"I'm not sure this is still Queens..."

"There must be a place we can wait on line for an hour before eating."

"Stop smiling. You're downtown."

"At first I was really angry they were erecting a building right smack up against mine."

"In New York, we wouldn't call this quick."

"I'm telling you, Manhattan is _over_."

"They're marinated in hot water for six hours."

"Nope....I can't make any sense out of that at all."

"Just when you're about to lose faith in humanity, you see
Shakespeare in the Park."

"We must be in the Village."

"It was worth waiting four months for a reservation."

THE REJECTS
I ♠ NY
I ♦ NY
I ♣ NY
R. Chast

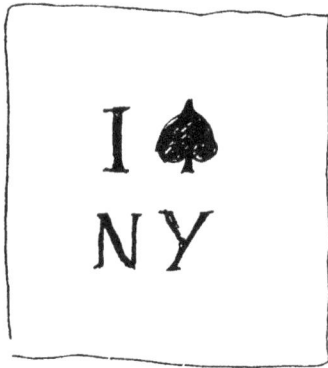

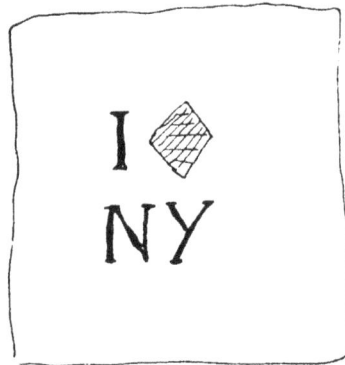

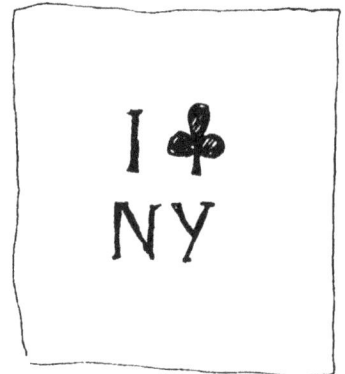

"Keep in mind, this all counts as screen time."

THE ILLUMINATI OF THE SUBWAY

Has never waited more than fifteen seconds for a train.

Owns one of those "bottomless" MetroCards.

The Ⓛ may not run for YOU...but it will for _HER_.

R. Chr

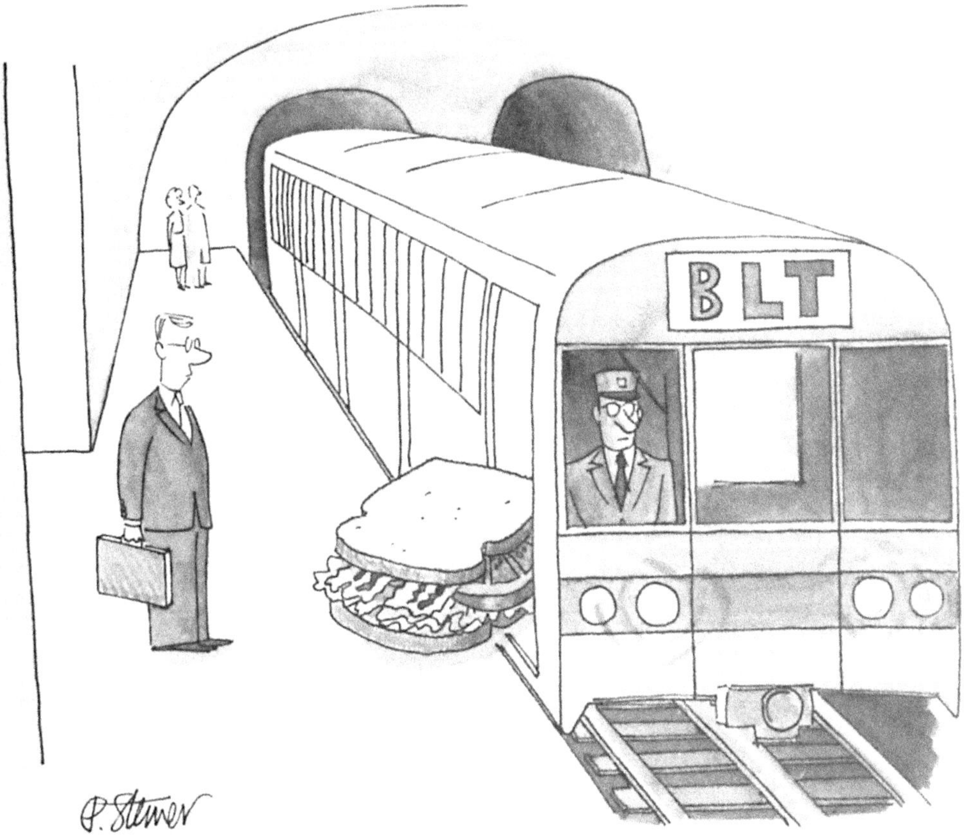
BLT
P. Steiner

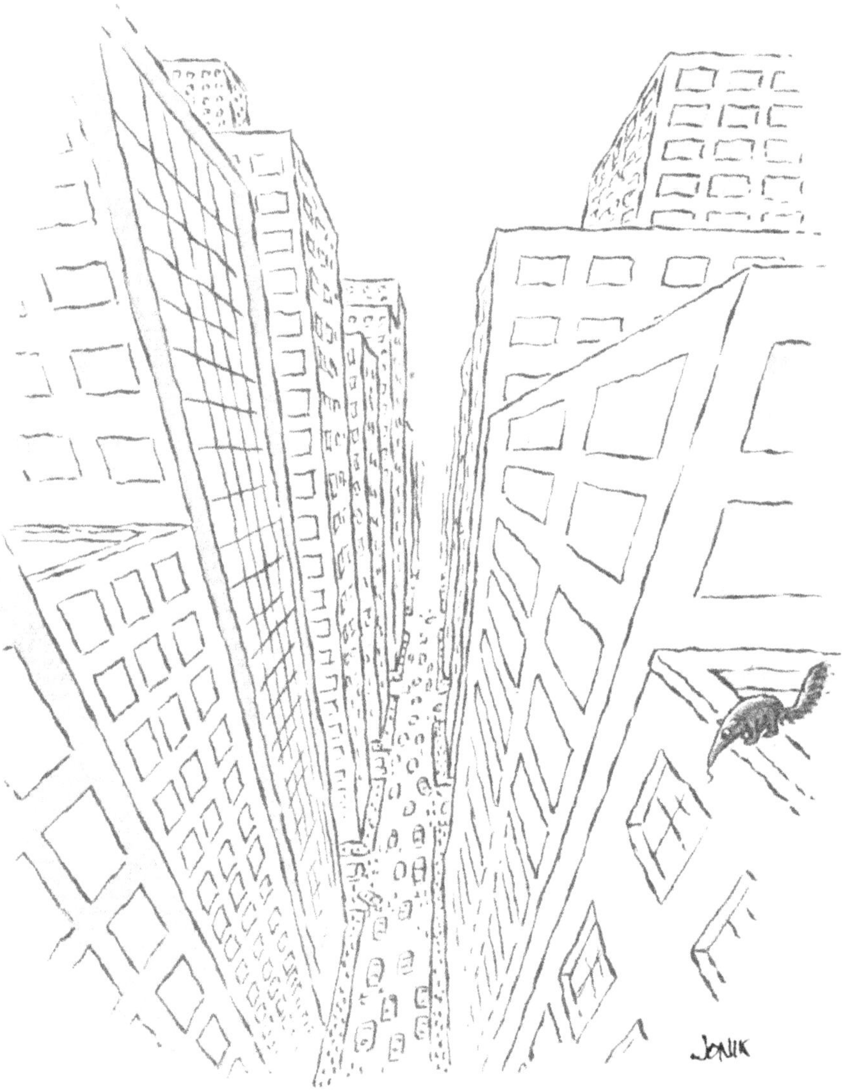
JONIK

s.MORRISSETTE

"I've been to cities other than New York. They're cute."

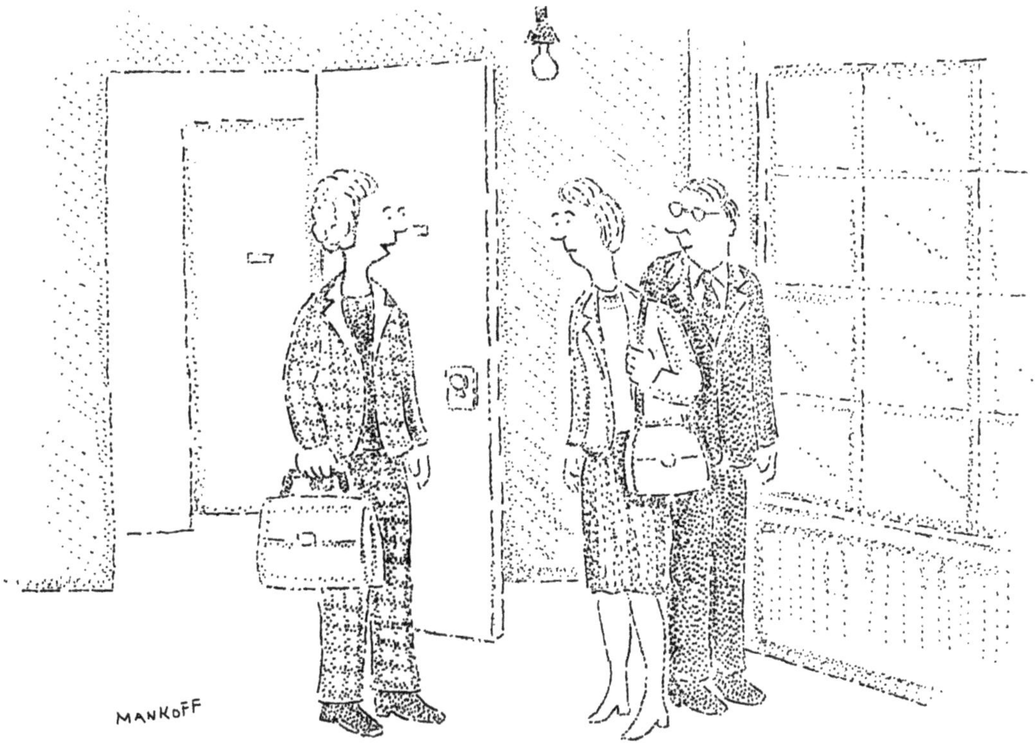
MANKOFF

"No, it's not prewar—yet."

"Because you're not naked, and you're not a cowboy, that's why!"

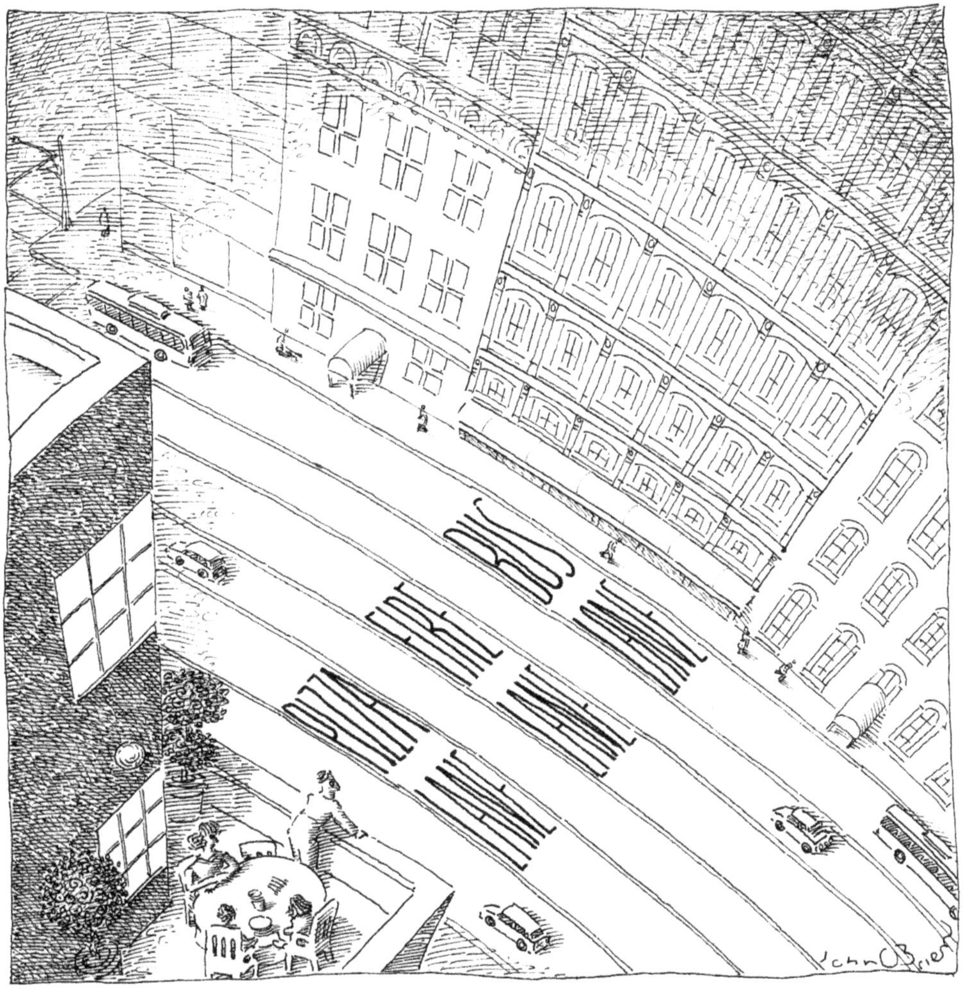
BUS LANE
BIKE LANE

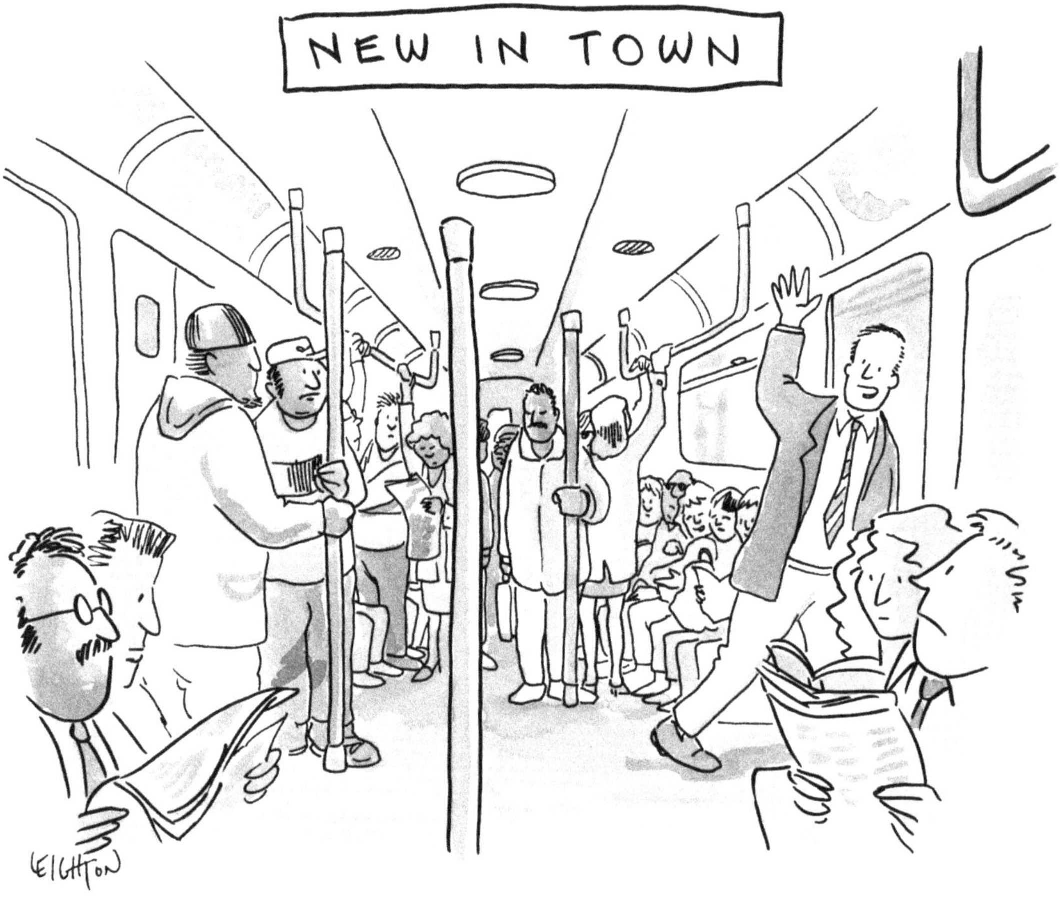
NEW IN TOWN
LEIGHTON

"Goodbye, everybody!"

The New York Review of Weather

TABLE OF CONTENTS

R.Clf

"Don't argue with me. The FDR will be faster!"

"Hey, folks – assuming everyone is on board, and barring any unforeseen technical glitches—it's showtime."

ENTERING
NEW YORK CITY
AN URBAN MYTH.

NICK DOWNES

"*Attention passengers, this train will be running express to whichever stop is after yours.*"

ENTERING
NEW YORK CITY
RECOMPRESS

S.GROSS

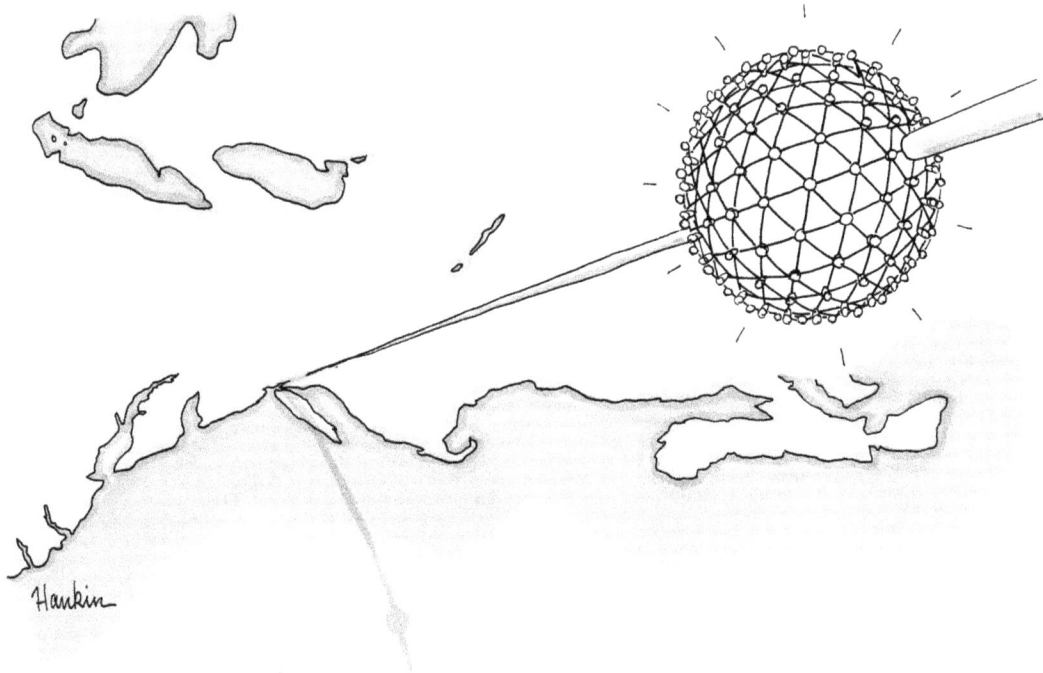

SIX MONTHS BEFORE NEW YEAR'S EVE

"It's New York. It wants you back."

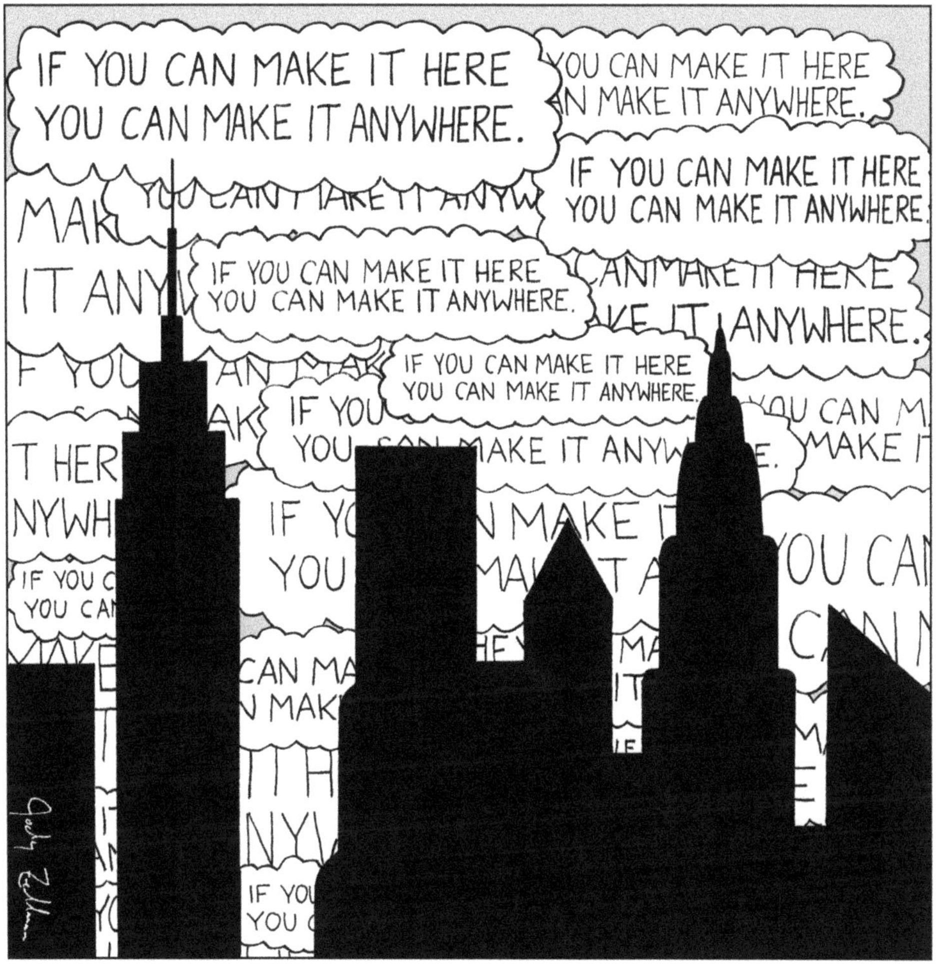
IF YOU CAN MAKE IT HERE
YOU CAN MAKE IT ANYWHERE.
IF YOU CAN MAKE IT HERE
YOU CAN MAKE IT ANYWHERE.
IF YOU CAN MAKE IT HERE
YOU CAN MAKE IT ANYWHERE.
IF YOU CAN MAKE IT HERE
YOU CAN MAKE IT ANYWHERE.

"I really prefer the quiet rhythms of the sewers to the hustle and bustle of the subways."

ENTERING
NEW YORK CITY
—
CHECK IT OUT

MANKOFF

"To me, the Hudson is much more than a river—it's a moat."

AS SEEN
ON THE
CORNER OF
34ᵀᴴ ST. &
MADISON

ZIEGLER

"Remember, if we get split up, take the A
to 42nd, transfer to the Brooklyn bound
2, get off at Eastern Parkway and buy a
ticket for the Brooklyn Museum and make
sure to tell them you're under three."

"I flew South once. Couldn't <u>buy</u> a decent soft pretzel."

"*Good luck getting a sandwich at this hour in L.A.*"

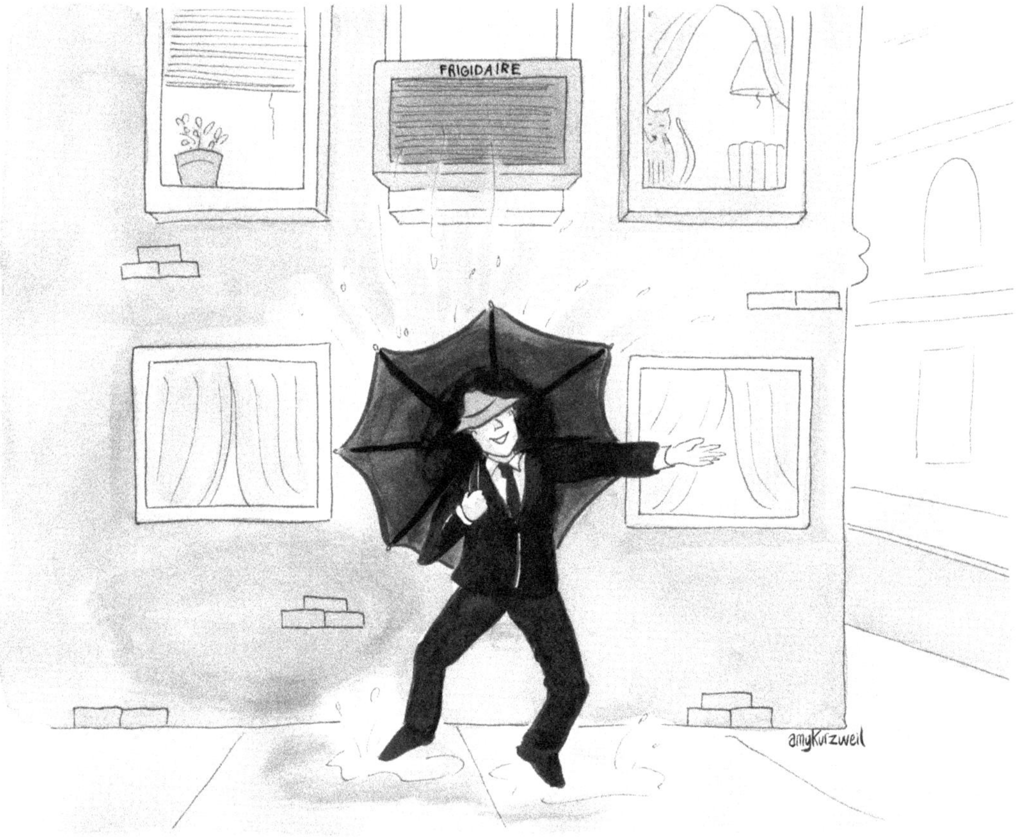
FRIGIDAIRE
amyKurzweil

"Sorry, this block is closed for filming a gritty,
hard-edged tale of passion and violence."

"Anywhere down there would be great."

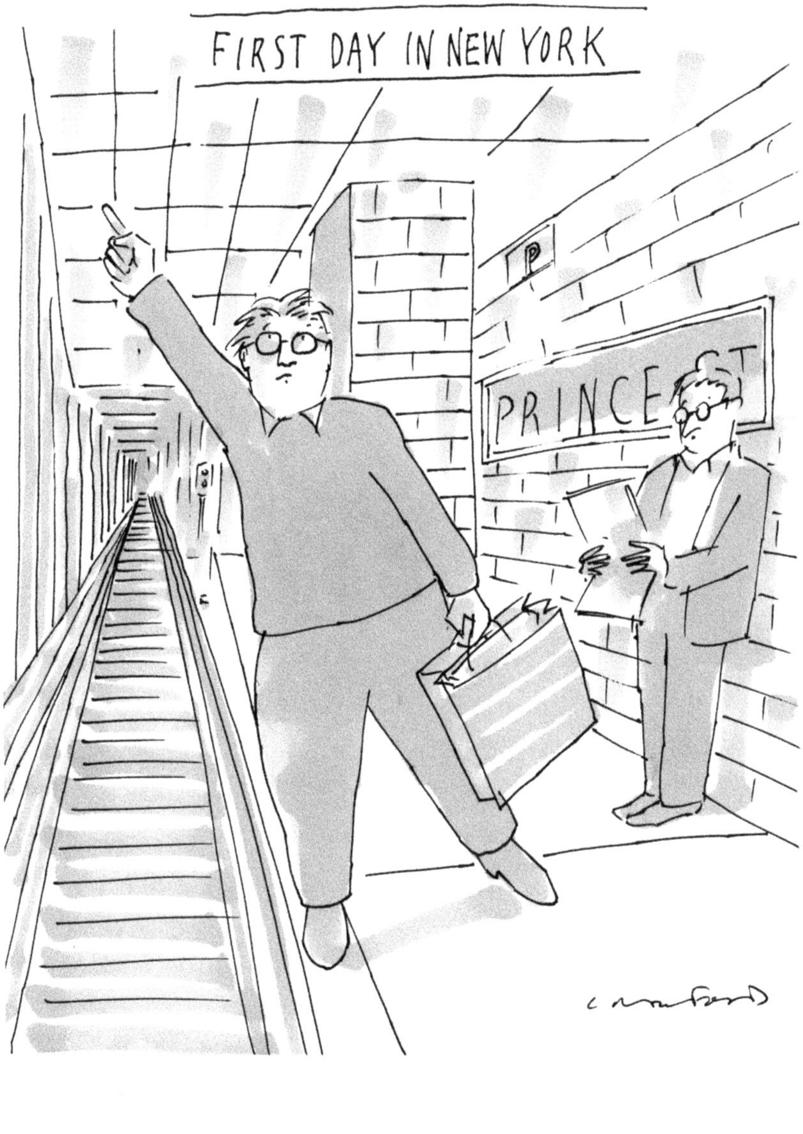
FIRST DAY IN NEW YORK
P
PRINCE ST

"*Take heed! For your journey is filled with long delays and unexpected service charges!*"

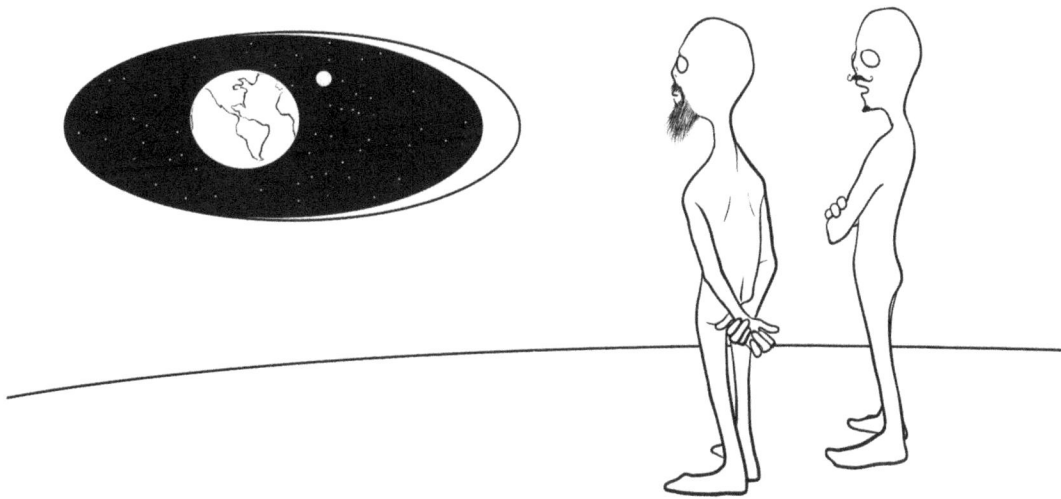

"First stop: Brooklyn."

GREGORY

52

"I dunno. The city looked so much better on Instagram."

NEW FROM NEW YORK CANDLE CO.

OLDE HALLWAY

6th AVENUE

Store

Let the scent of stuffed cabbage, some sort of curry thing, and Janitor-in-a-Drum pervade your senses.

Indulge in the aroma of burnt pretzel and bus exhaust, graced with high notes of coffee and marijuana.

Imagine an enormous vat into which all the world's perfumes have been poured and blended into one.

R. Chst

"This is a side of Manhattan you don't often see."

"Do you think the people at the higher rooftop
bar are having more fun?"

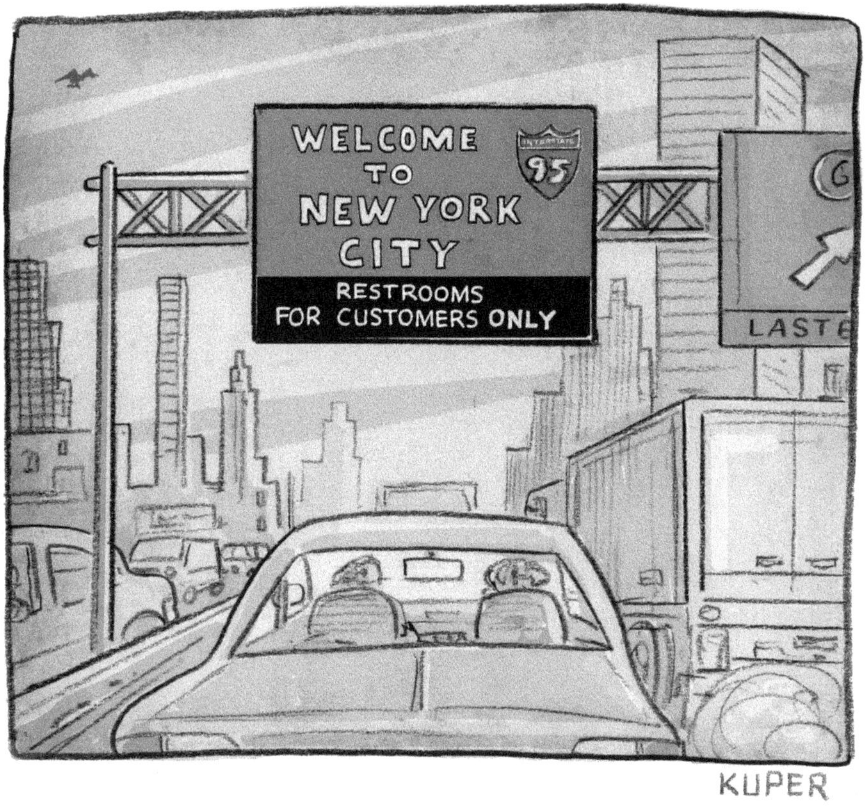
WELCOME TO NEW YORK CITY
95
RESTROOMS FOR CUSTOMERS ONLY
KUPER

"Of course—we wait forever, then come at the same time."

TOURISTS from SPACE

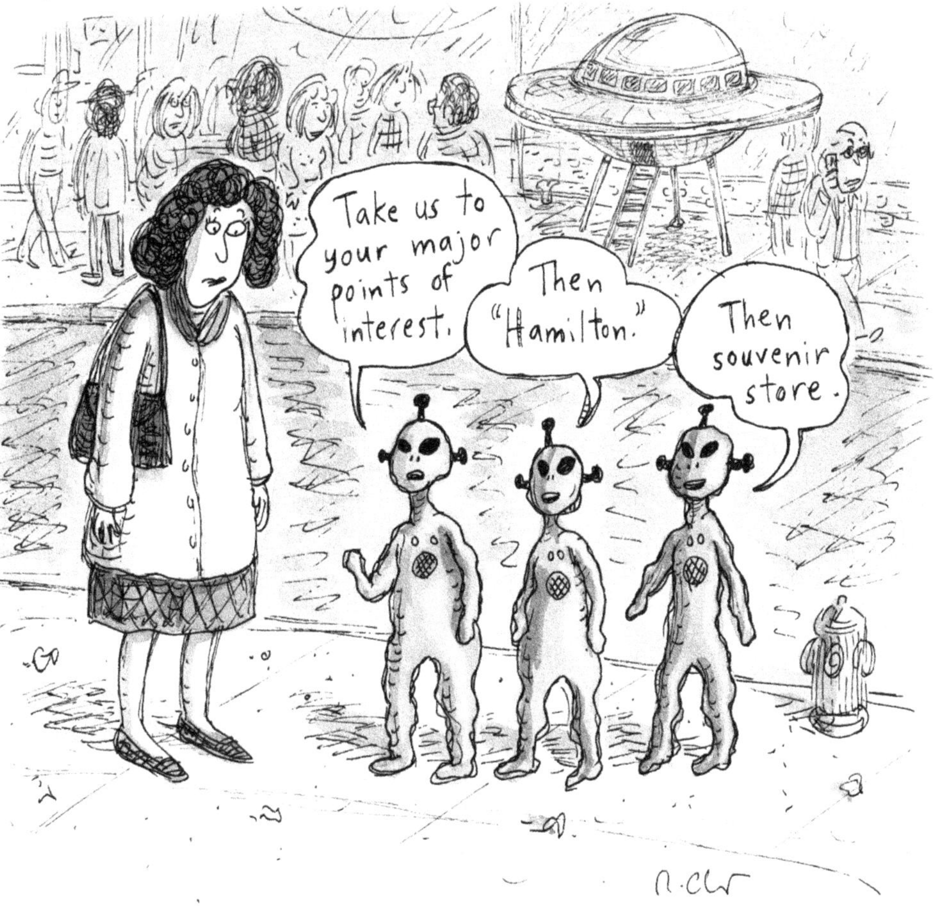
Take us to your major points of interest.
Then "Hamilton."
Then souvenir store.

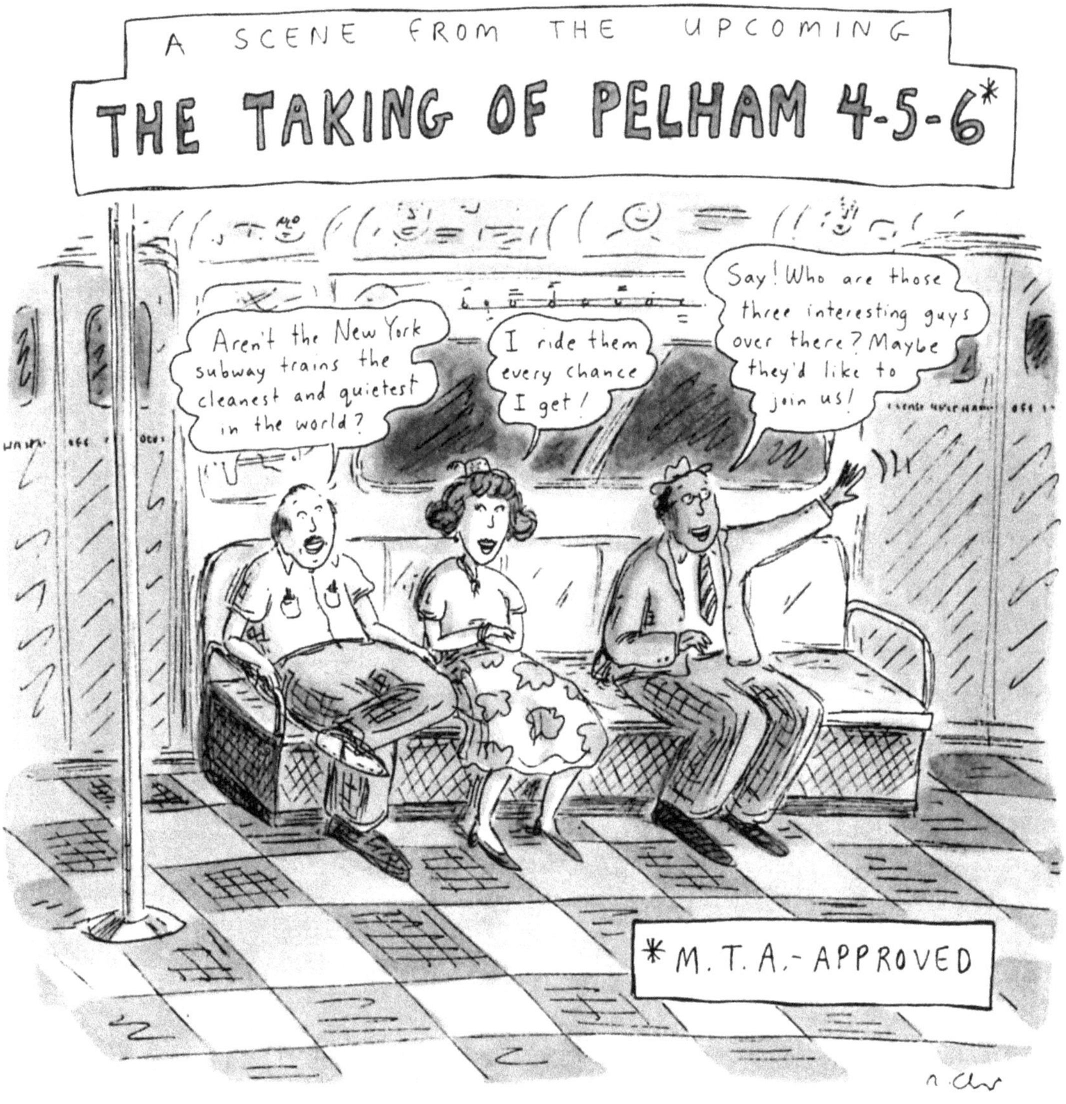
A SCENE FROM THE UPCOMING
THE TAKING OF PELHAM 4-5-6*
Aren't the New York subway trains the cleanest and quietest in the world?
I ride them every chance I get!
Say! Who are those three interesting guys over there? Maybe they'd like to join us!
*M.T.A.-APPROVED

"*Well, like they say—if you don't like New York weather, wait twenty years till it's all underwater.*"

"He's been to the city exactly once."

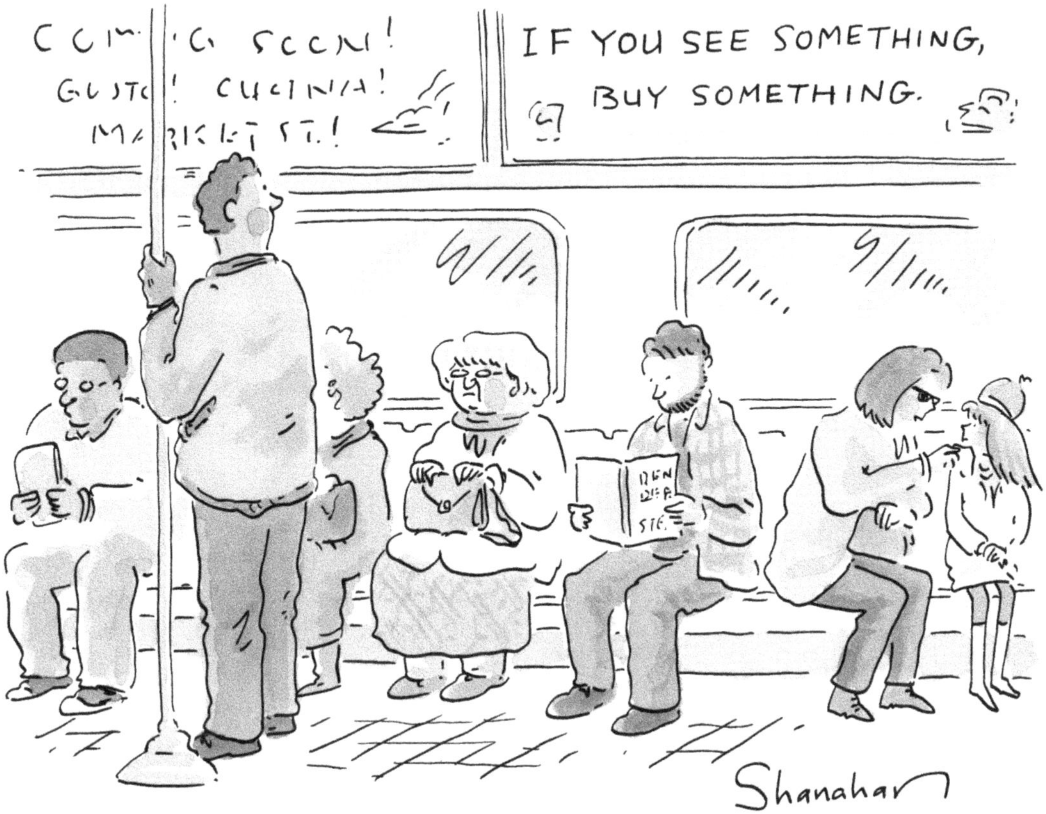
IF YOU SEE SOMETHING,
BUY SOMETHING.
Shanahan

HOAX ETHNIC FOOD

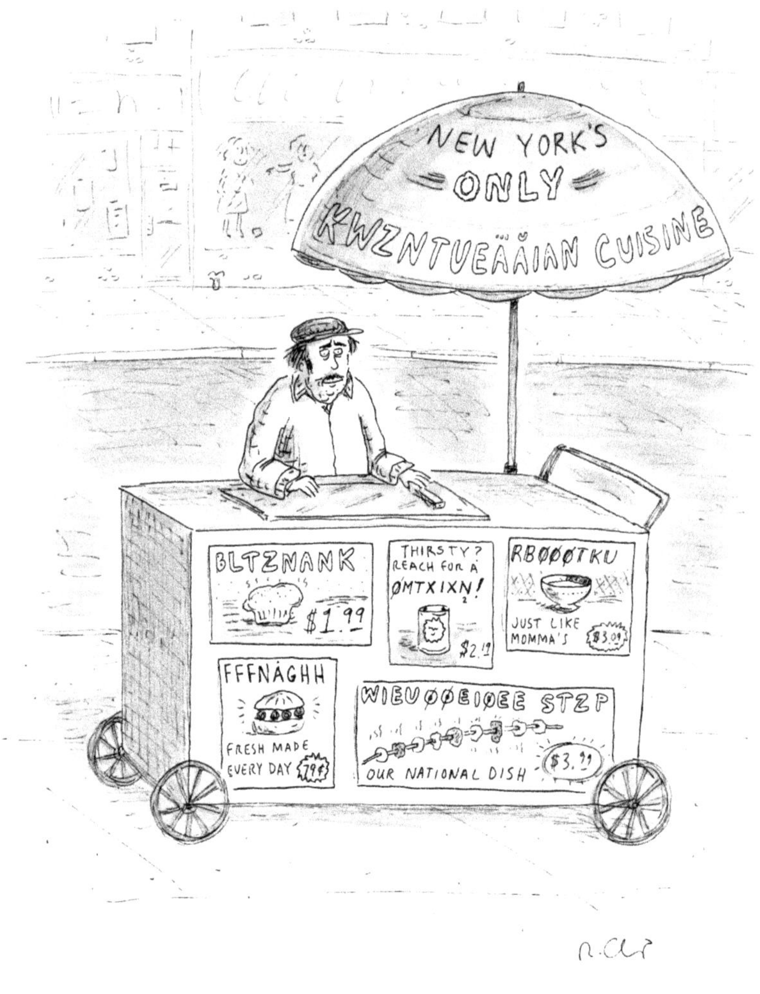
NEW YORK'S
ONLY
KWZNTUEÄÄIAN CUISINE
BLTZNANK
$1.99
THIRSTY? REACH FOR A ØMTXIXN!
$2.19
RBØØØTKU
JUST LIKE MOMMA'S
$3.09
FFFNÄGHH
FRESH MADE EVERY DAY
79¢
WIEUØØEIØEE STZP
OUR NATIONAL DISH
$3.99

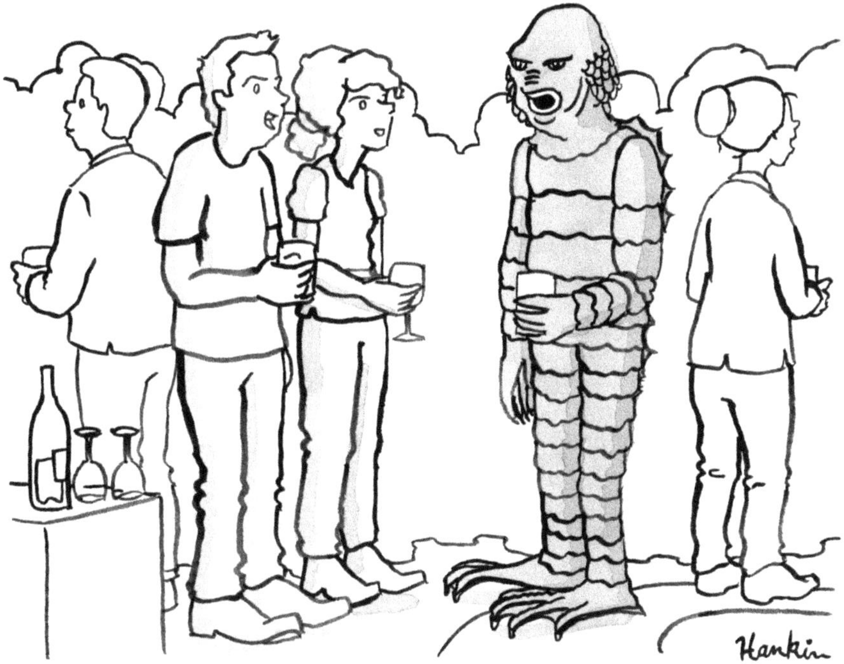
Hankin

"I grew up in St Louis and went to school in New Jersey and have been in Brooklyn ever-since, but sure, I guess technically I'm 'from' the Black Lagoon."

DRESSING FOR THE MANHATTAN CLIMATE

SUMMER IN
CENTRAL PARK

OR

WINTER IN
OVERHEATED
APARTMENT

FALL/WINTER IN
CENTRAL PARK

OR

SUMMER IN
OVER-AIR-CONDITIONED
OFFICE

CAJ·s

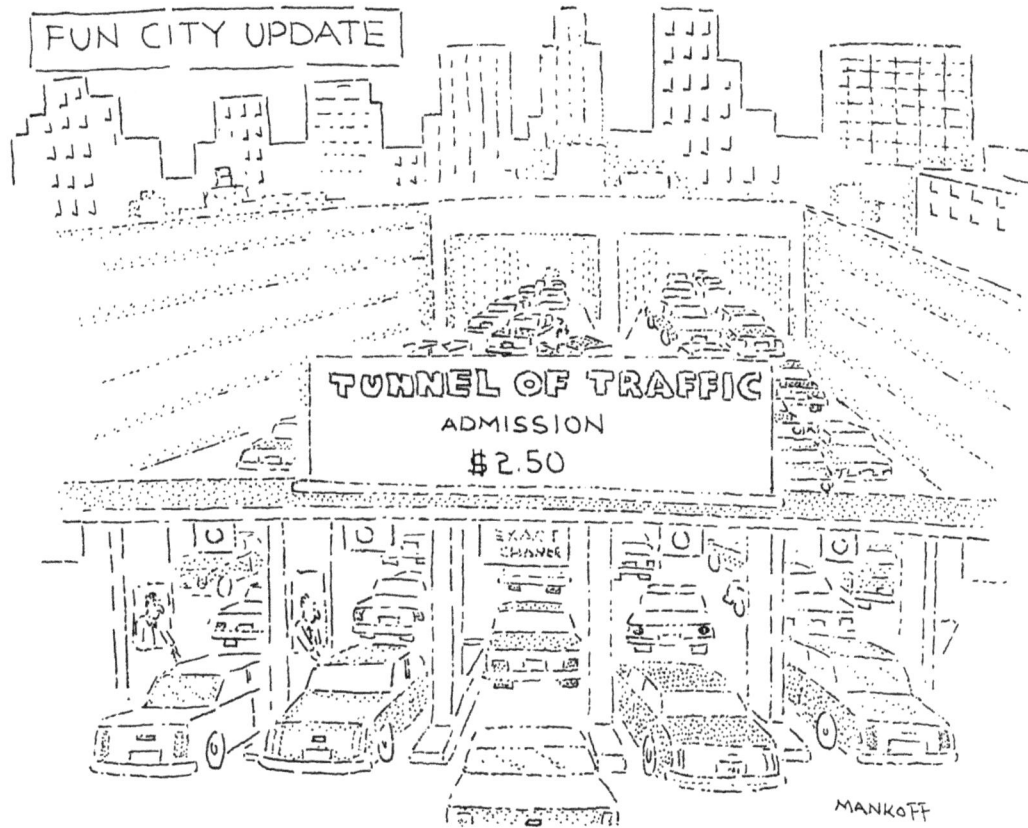

FUN CITY UPDATE

TUNNEL OF TRAFFIC
ADMISSION
$2.50

MANKOFF

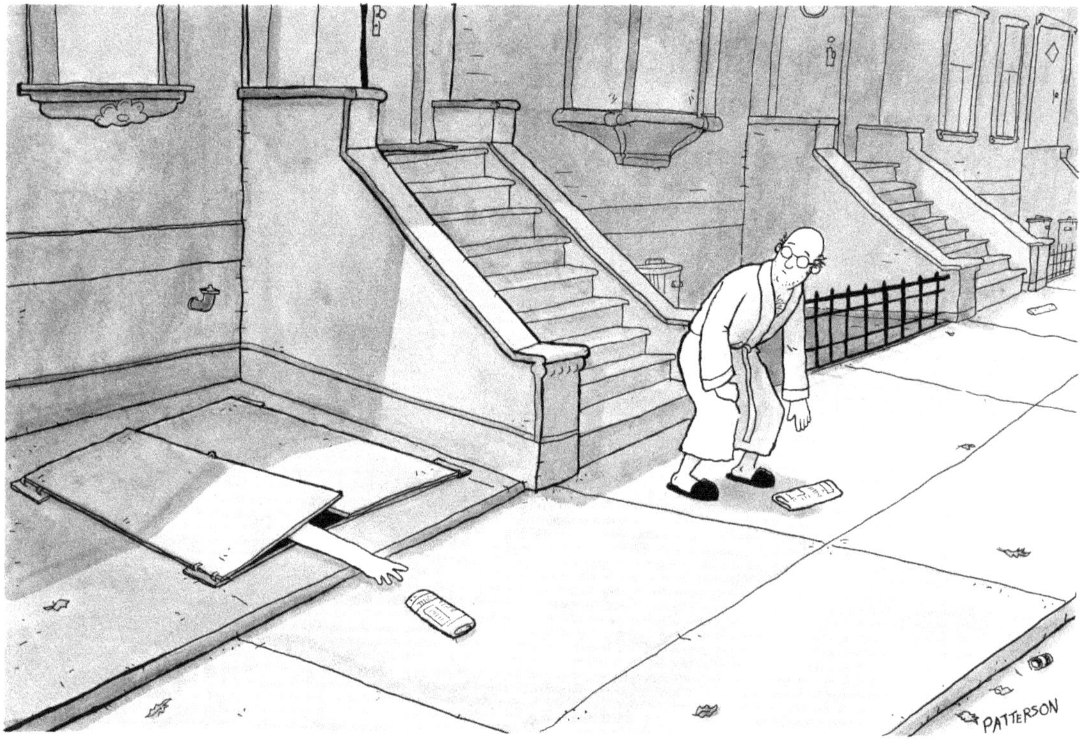
PATTERSON

"Until we hear different, it's Jersey's problem."

"I'm going to give you something to help you sleep."

"I told you we'd be better off taking Canal."

"It's not that I love New York. It's just that I hate everyplace else."

"The Hamptons were nice but it feels good to be back in the city."

Planned Service Changes

2 — The 2 train is going back to school to pursue a career in massage therapy.

F — The F train has accepted a position at another subway system. We wish it luck in future endeavors.

L — The L train is taking three years off to find itself.

"You see where Sixth Avenue meets Broadway?
That's where you want to be."

"Wow! This is just like the tv show I've spent my whole life emulating!"

WAKE THE EFF UP WITH
THE OFFICIAL NEW YORK CITY !!! ALARM !!! CLOCK
3:02
CHOOSE YOUR DISTRESS SIGNAL:
·CAR HORNS
·SIRENS
·BARKING
·HEAT PIPES
·MOUSE FEET
GUARANTEED TO DISTURB!
SUSANNA GOLDFINGER

"You can always spot the tourists."

"Isn't this nice?"

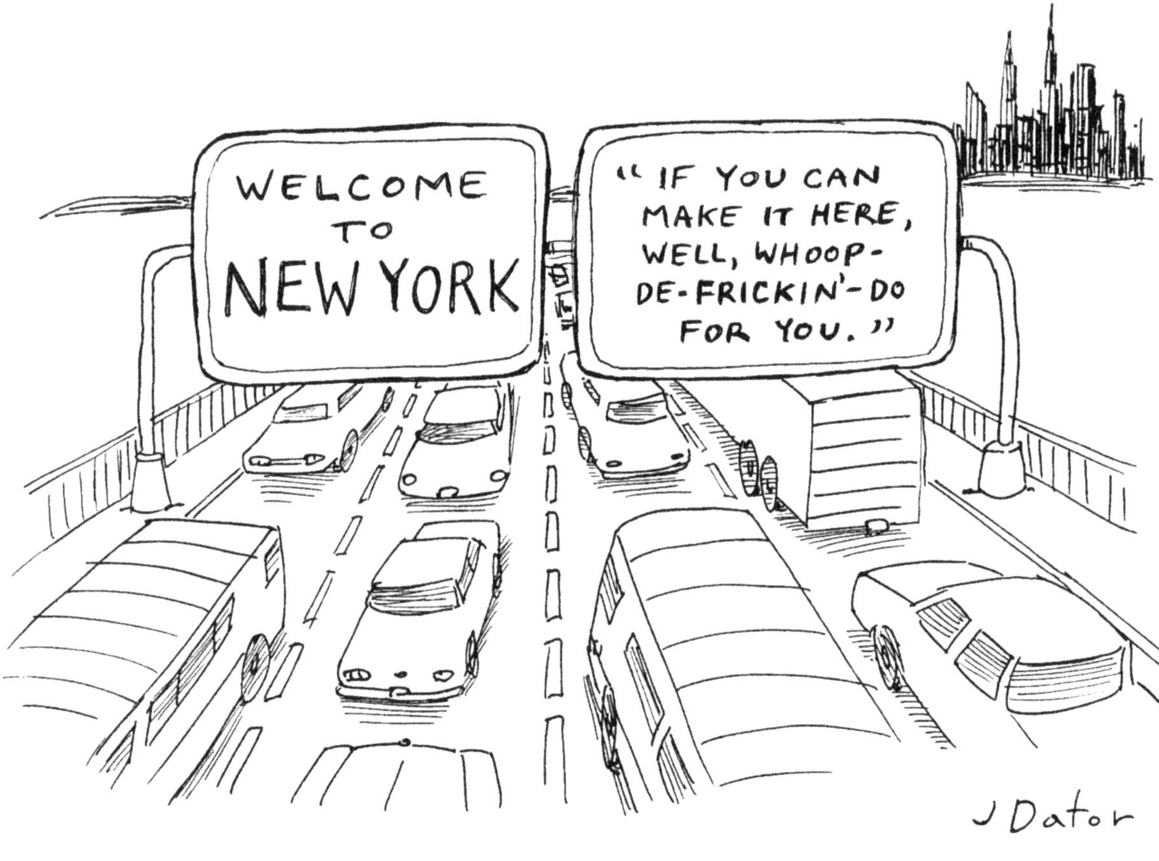
WELCOME TO NEW YORK
"IF YOU CAN MAKE IT HERE, WELL, WHOOP-DE-FRICKIN'-DO FOR YOU."
J Dator

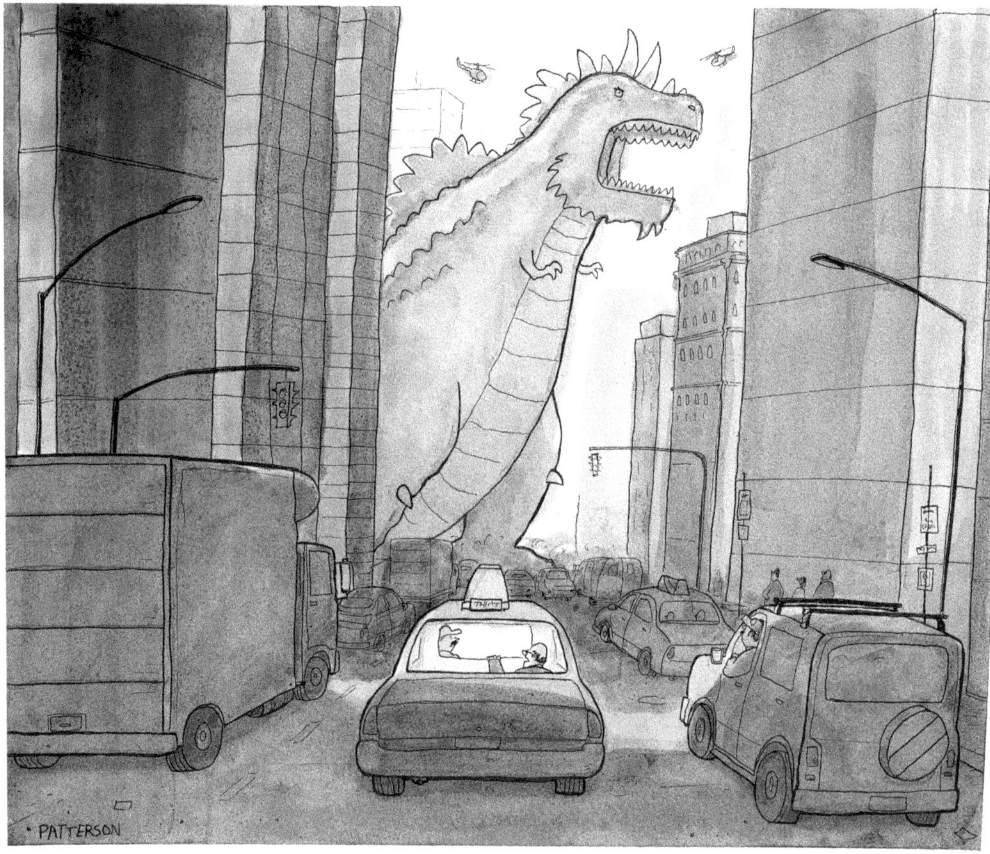
PATTERSON

"O.K., O.K., let's take the F.D.R."

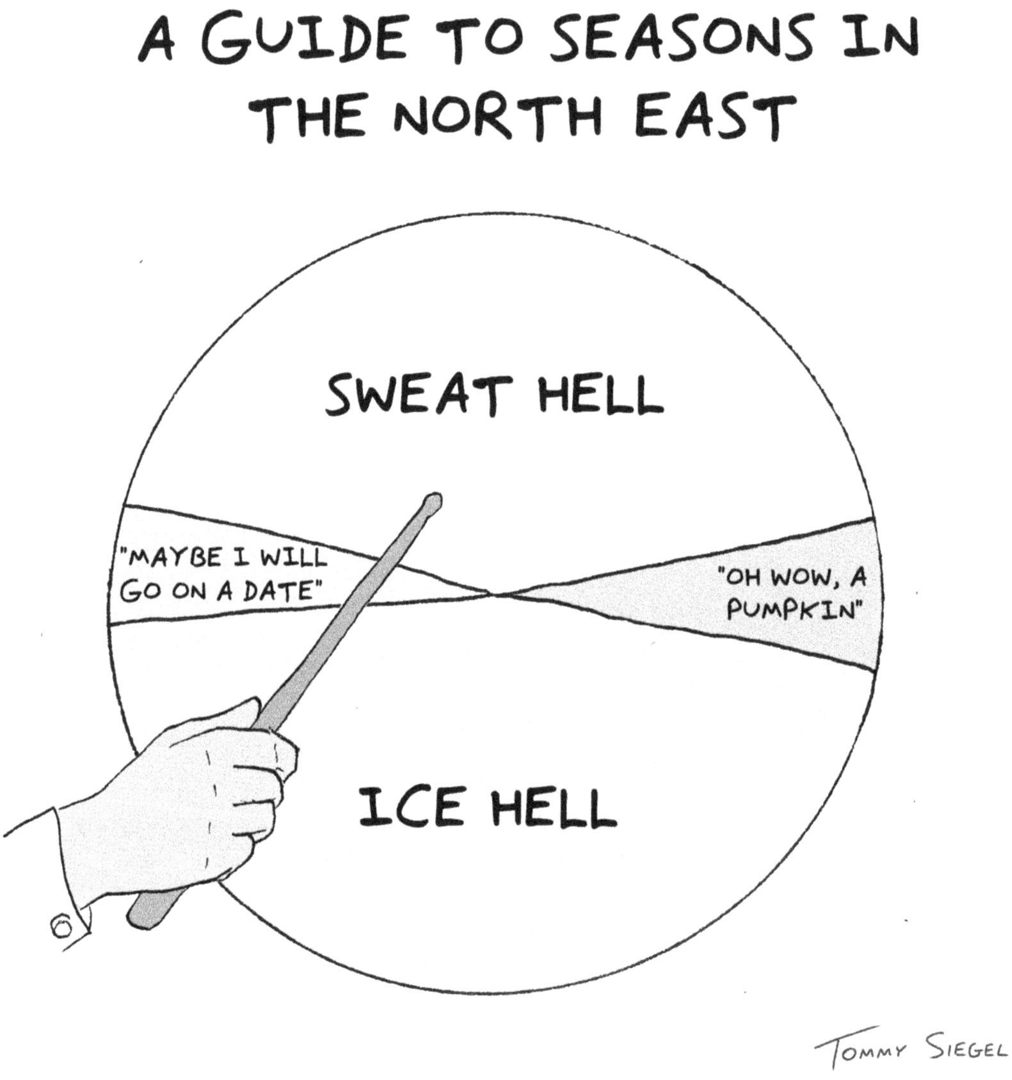
A GUIDE TO SEASONS IN THE NORTH EAST
SWEAT HELL
"MAYBE I WILL GO ON A DATE"
"OH WOW, A PUMPKIN"
ICE HELL
TOMMY SIEGEL

"Sometimes I come up here and think about the great meals I've eaten."

"*Nice to see him getting landmark status.*"

"Hey, is this great traffic, or what?"

Index of Artists

www.ingramcontent.com/pod-product-compliance
Lightning Source LLC
Chambersburg PA
CBHW040848100426
42813CB00015B/2741